NATURAL MARVELS

Worlds Beneath Our Feet

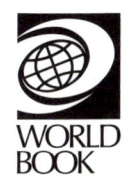

WORLD BOOK

World Book, Inc.
180 North LaSalle Street, Suite 900
Chicago, Illinois 60601
USA

For information about other World Book publications, please visit our website at www.worldbook.com or call 1-800-WORLDBK (967-5325).

For information about sales to schools and libraries, please call 1-800-975-3250 (United States) or 1-800-837-5365 (Canada).

© 2017 World Book, Inc. All rights reserved. This volume may not be reproduced in whole or in part in any form without prior written permission from the publisher. WORLD BOOK and the GLOBE DEVICE are registered trademarks or trademarks of World Book, Inc.

Library of Congress Cataloging-in-Publication Data

Title: Worlds beneath our feet.
Description: Chicago: World Book, Inc., a Scott Fetzer company, [2017] | Series: Natural marvels | Includes index.
Identifiers: LCCN 2016039128 | ISBN 9780716633716
Subjects: LCSH: Caves--Juvenile literature. | Mammoth Cave (Ky.)--Juvenile literature. | Skocjan Caves (Slovenia)--Juvenile literature. | Crystals, Cave of (Mexico)--Juvenile literature.
Classification: LCC GB601.2 .W67 2017 | DDC 551.44/7--dc23
LC record available at https://lccn.loc.gov/2016039128

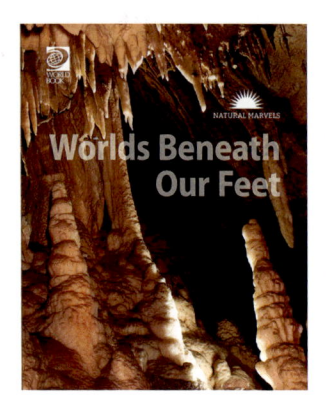

Over eons, the forces of nature have sculpted Earth in certain locations to create majestic landscapes of great beauty. Some of the most spectacular landforms are featured in this series of books. This image shows some of the strange rock formations at Mammoth Cave National Park in the United States.

This edition:
ISBN: 978-0-7166-3371-6 (hc.)
ISBN: 978-0-7166-3363-1 (set, hc.)

Also available as:
ISBN: 978-0-7166-3380-8
(e-book, EPUB3)

Printed in China by Shenzhen Wing King Tong Paper Products Co., Ltd. Shenzhen, Guangdong
1st printing March 2017

STAFF

Writer: Daniel Kenis

Executive Committee

President
Jim O'Rourke

Vice President and Editor in Chief
Paul A. Kobasa

Vice President, Finance
Donald D. Keller

Vice President, Marketing
Jean Lin

Vice President, International Sales
Maksim Rutenberg

Director, Human Resources
Bev Ecker

Editorial

Director, Digital and Print Content Development
Emily Kline

Editor, Digital and Print Content Development
Kendra Muntz

Manager, Science
Jeff De La Rosa

Editors, Science
William D. Adams
Nicholas V. Kilzer

Administrative Assistant, Digital and Print Content Development
Ethel Matthews

Manager, Contracts & Compliance (Rights & Permissions)
Loranne K. Shields

Manager, Indexing Services
David Pofelski

Graphics and Design

Senior Art Director
Tom Evans

Senior Designer
Don Di Sante

Media Editor
Rosalia Bledsoe

Senior Cartographer
John M. Rejba

Manufacturing/Production

Production/Technology Manager
Anne Fritzinger

Proofreader
Nathalie Strassheim

Table of Contents

Introduction 4

Mammoth Cave 6

Where Is Mammoth Cave and What's Special About It? 8

How Mammoth Cave Formed 10

Spelunking Speak 12

Cave Creatures.. 14

Mammoth Cave and Explorers 18

Škocjan Caves 20

Where Are the Škocjan Caves and What's Special About Them? 22

A Real-Life River Styx 24

Škocjan and Geology 26

Life in the Škocjan Caves 28

The Cave of the Crystals 30

Where Is the Cave of the Crystals and What's Special About It? 32

How Did Those Crystals Get So Big? 34

Otherworldly Life 36

Glossary 38

Find Out More 39

Index 40

Glossary There is a glossary of terms on page 38. Terms defined in the glossary are in type **that looks like this** on their first appearance on any spread (two facing pages). Words that are difficult to say are followed by a pronunciation (*pruh NUHN see AY shuhn*) the first time they are used.

Introduction

If you've never been inside a cave, you've probably never experienced true darkness. The night is dark, but not *totally* dark. The stars and moon still shine—not to mention the lights in our houses and along our streets. Even in a windowless room, with a towel stuffed under the door, some light usually gets in. But deep inside a cave, the darkness is complete. Whether your eyes are open or closed, what you see is the same—nothing.

Many people are afraid of the dark. Perhaps that is why such frightening stories are told about caves. In many ancient **myths,** for example, spirits of the dead roam a cavelike underworld. In other stories, monsters lurk in caves.

These myths and legends are not often so far from the truth. Creatures called **troglobites** (*trog luh bahytz*)—pale, eyeless versions of animals from the surface— do lurk in caves. And, while caves do not hold dead spirits, many caves are as dark and silent as tombs.

This book covers three of the world's most impressive caves. In the eastern United States, Mammoth Cave of Kentucky is part of the longest cave system ever explored. In the central European country of Slovenia, a vast underground canyon lies within the Škocjan (*shkoh TSAYHN*) Cave. And Mexico's Cave of the Crystals is full of, as you would guess, **crystals**— *gigantic* crystals, the size of towers.

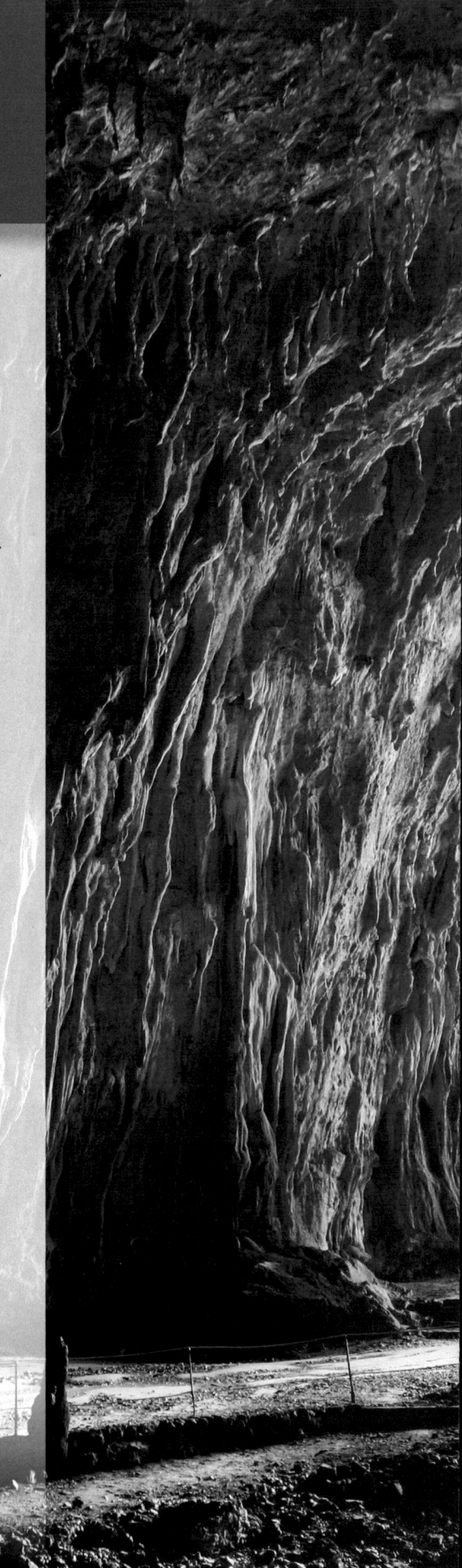

Arctic Ocean

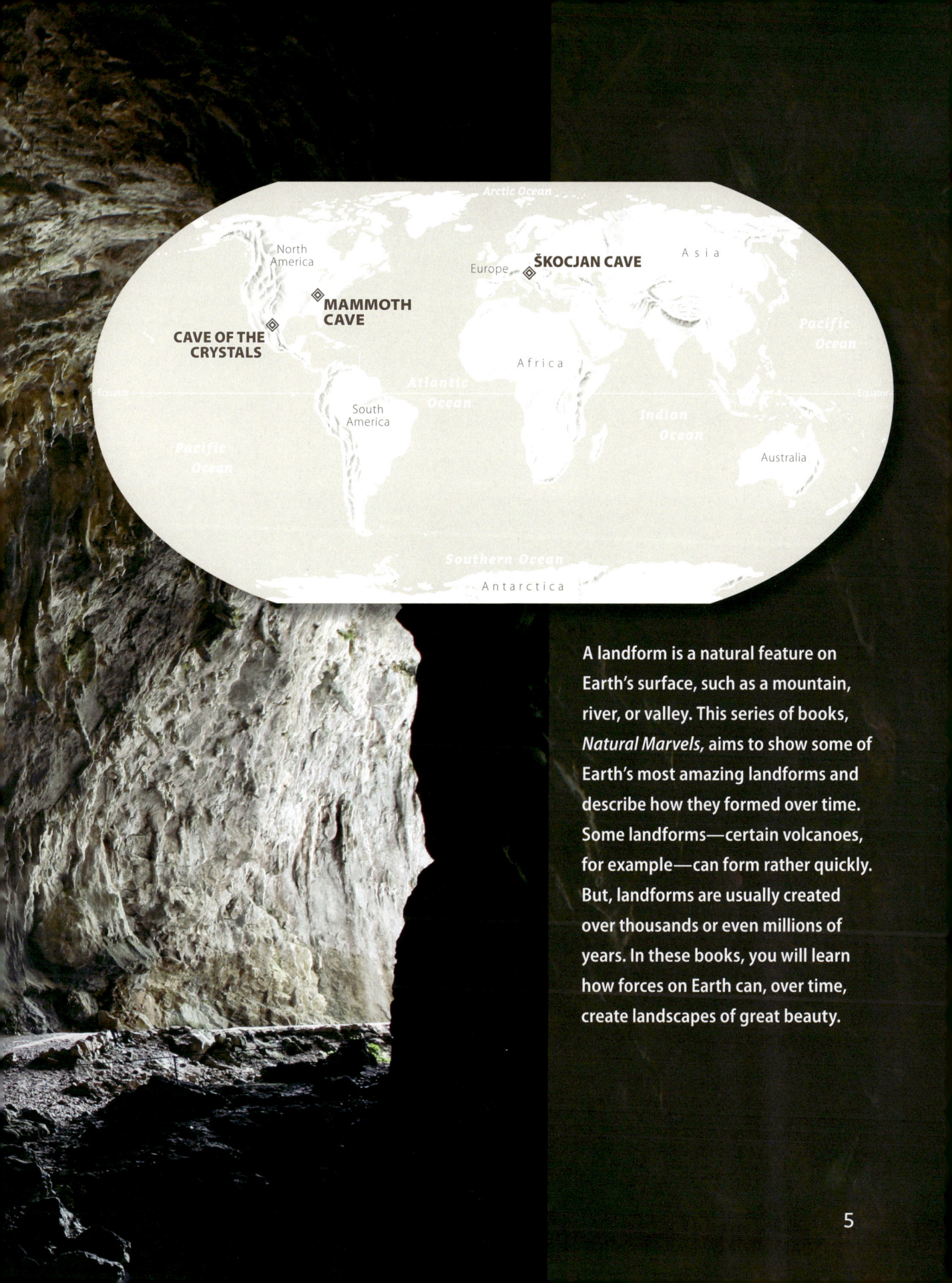

North America — ◇ MAMMOTH CAVE
◇ CAVE OF THE CRYSTALS
Europe — ◇ ŠKOCJAN CAVE
Asia
Africa
South America
Atlantic Ocean
Pacific Ocean
Indian Ocean
Australia
Equator
Southern Ocean
Antarctica

A landform is a natural feature on Earth's surface, such as a mountain, river, or valley. This series of books, *Natural Marvels,* aims to show some of Earth's most amazing landforms and describe how they formed over time. Some landforms—certain volcanoes, for example—can form rather quickly. But, landforms are usually created over thousands or even millions of years. In these books, you will learn how forces on Earth can, over time, create landscapes of great beauty.

Mammoth Cave

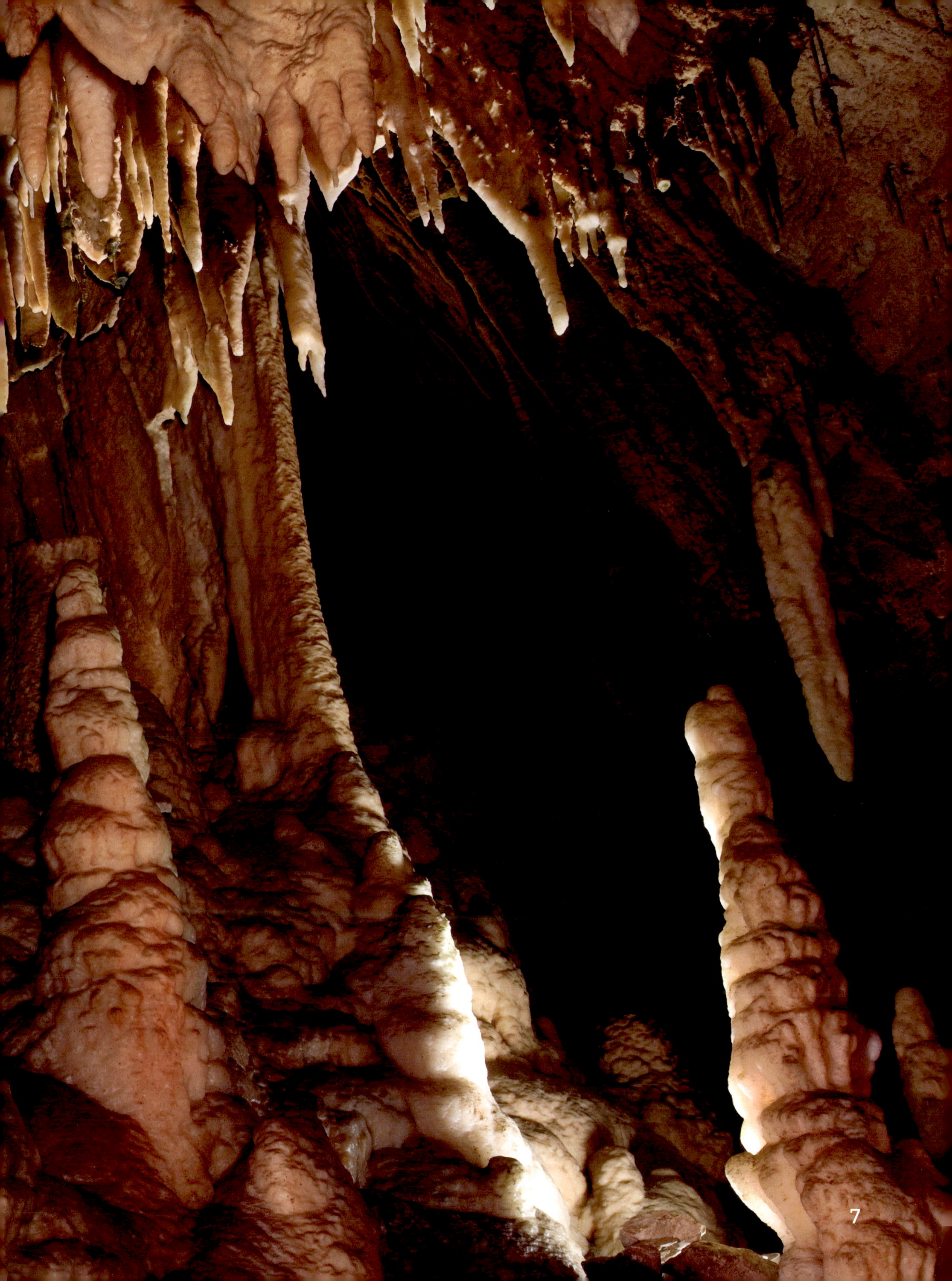

Where Is Mammoth Cave and What's Special About It?

Mammoth Cave lies in the central part of the U.S. state of Kentucky. It is often called one of the wonders of the *Western Hemisphere* (the half of the world with North and South America). Why? Because it's absolutely enormous! *Mammoth*, in fact, is another word for *big*. Mammoth Cave forms part of a system that snakes under Earth for over 400 miles (640 kilometers). Its lowest level lies 360 feet (110 meters) below the surface.

The cave holds a hidden world of narrow tunnels and giant halls. Cave explorers, called **spelunkers** (*spih LUHNG kuhrs*), are still finding new tunnels and caverns in this underworld maze. Water drips and flows throughout Mammoth Cave, forming rivers, lakes, and waterfalls. Echo River, the biggest waterway inside the cave system, is 60 feet (18 meters) wide at points, and up to 25 feet (8 meters) deep.

Strange rock formations called **speleothems** (*speel yuh thehmz*) line the walls, floors, and ceilings. Some formations resemble flowers or trees. Others have a liquid appearance, like waterfalls made of solid rock. Because the cave system is so big, it contains nearly every kind of known speleothem. In addition, more kinds of **troglobites** live in Mammoth than any other cave.

Its size and features make Mammoth Cave a popular tourist attraction. The cave system forms part of Mammoth Cave National Park.

This map of the Mammoth Cave system shows how large the cave is. **Speleologists** *(spee lee OL uh jihsts, scientists who study caves) are still finding new parts of the cave today.*

9

How Mammoth Cave Formed

Mammoth Cave lies in a region made mostly of **limestone** rock. Limestone's unique characteristics explain how Mammoth Cave—and many other caves around the world—formed over time.

Rock seems solid and unchanging. But solid substances can *dissolve* (*dih ZOLV, break down*) in water. Just look at what happens when you pour water on solid table salt. Limestone does not dissolve nearly as quickly as salt in water. But it does dissolve faster than many other types of rock.

Over thousands of years, water trickles down through cracks in Earth's surface. The water collects underground, forming a **water table.** As water flows into and around the water table, it dissolves the surrounding limestone. This process leaves behind passages, chambers, and pits in the rock. Such areas of Earth, formed of soft rock with abundant water, are called **karst** formations. In these karst formations, slowly but surely, caves are often created.

Eventually, the water table may drop below the level of the cave. Air fills the gaps left by the water's dissolving action. Scientists believe Mammoth Cave formed in this way over millions of years. Surface water continues to seep and drip into Mammoth Cave. This water contains dissolved limestone and other minerals. As the water enters the cave, some of the dissolved minerals "stick" to the rock. In this way, many striking **speleothems** are created.

*Speleothems in the **Drapery** Room in Mammoth Cave.*

Spelunking Speak

The best-known kinds of **speleothems** are stalactites and stalagmites (above). **Stalactites** are iciclelike formations that hang from the ceiling of a cave. **Stalagmites** are pillars that rise from the floor. A stalactite and a stalagmite may join and form a column.

Drapery (below) consists of thin sheets of rock that hang from the ceiling. Draperies form much like stalactites do.

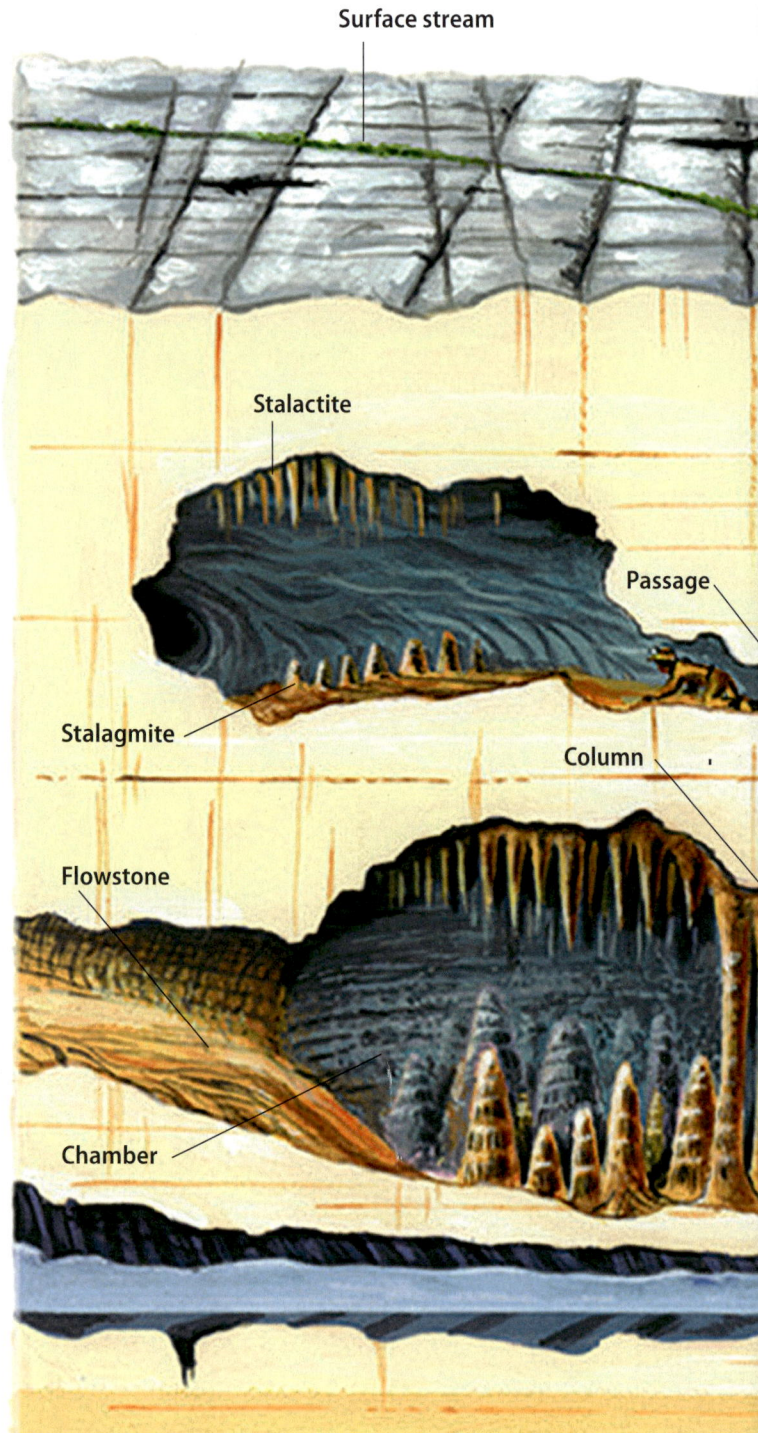

Surface stream

Stalactite

Passage

Stalagmite

Column

Flowstone

Chamber

12

Gypsum *flowers (top right) are one crystal form of the mineral gypsum.*

Helictites (hehl ihk tytz, bottom right) are strangely twisted speleothems that grow from the walls, ceiling, or floor of a cave or from other rock formations.

Waterfall

Sinkhole

Pit

Helictites

Drapery

Limestone

Pool

Underground stream

Water table

13

Cave Creatures

No woolly mammoths ever lived in Mammoth Cave, but plenty of other fascinating creatures make their home there. The dark interior of the cave forms a unique **habitat.** Plants can grow only in places with sunlight. Some plants grow around the cave's entrances, but in the deepest areas of a cave, no plants can survive.

Not all cave dwellers spend their whole lives in the dark. Bats mostly use Mammoth Cave for shelter. At night, they fly out and hunt for insects. Bat droppings, called *guano* (*GWAH noh*), once formed an important food source for other Mammoth Cave creatures. But far fewer bats live in Mammoth Cave than in the past.

A harvestman (above) looks like, and is related to, spiders, but it is not a spider. Cave harvestmen are specially suited for life in the dark—they have no eyes.

An Indiana bat (left) roosts (hangs from the ceiling to sleep). This bat is an endangered species.

The cave cricket is a particularly important animal at Mammoth Cave. This cricket has long, spindly legs and *antennae* (feelers), which it uses to sense its dark surroundings. It feeds mostly outside the cave, but sleeps inside the cave entrance. Its waste and eggs provide food for animals that live deeper inside Mammoth Cave. In this way, the cave cricket acts a bit like a food delivery service for **troglobites**—animals that never leave the darkness.

Cave crickets use their antennae to feel in the dark.

Cave Creatures *continued from previous page*

Troglobites live in total darkness. Deep inside a cave, no plants can grow. No wind blows, and the temperature never changes much. A troglobite's life probably seems like a gloomy existence—to us humans. But like all living things, troglobites are **adapted** to their surroundings. Their bodies have changed over a long time to thrive in the underworld. Troglobites don't *need* to see anything. Instead, they rely on highly developed senses of smell or touch.

The cavefish (top photo at right) is a well-known troglobite. These eyeless creatures live in the Echo River. They are about 3 inches (8 centimeters) long. Their skin is pale pink. The pink color comes from their blood, which shows through their flesh. Scientists think the ancestors of the cavefish were normal fish with eyes. After ages in darkness, new generations of cavefish grew smaller and less useful eyes, until their eyes simply did not grow at all. The cavefish grows fleshy bumps on its body and head. These bumps give the fish a good sense of touch, so it can sense its surroundings without sight.

Other blind creatures living in Mammoth Cave include the cave beetle, cave shrimp, and cave crayfish. All of these troglobites rely on touch to make their way in the darkness.

Cavefish

Kentucky cave shrimp

Cave millipede

The animals shown on this page are so well adapted to living in caves that they would struggle to survive outside of them. They all are eyeless creatures that depend on smell and touch to survive.

Mammoth Cave and Explorers

People have been exploring Mammoth Cave for thousands of years. The first **spelunkers** in the cave were Native Americans. Their moccasins, tools, torches, and the remains of *mummies* (preserved dead bodies) have been found inside the cave.

By the late 1700's, the first European settlers visited Mammoth Cave. During the War of 1812, people mined the cave for a natural mineral called saltpeter, an ingredient for making gunpowder. After the war ended, the cave became a public showplace.

One of the most important Mammoth Cave explorers was an African American slave named Stephen Bishop. He served as a guide. But he wasn't afraid to risk his life venturing into new areas of the underground maze. Bishop discovered the Echo River and the blind cavefish that live in it. He famously described Mammoth Cave as "grand, gloomy, and peculiar."

Stephen Bishop (1821-1857) (left) was one of the first people to map the cave and named many of the cave's features. He was freed from slavery in 1856.

THE DANGERS OF SPELUNKING

Cave exploring is dangerous. One particularly unlucky spelunker was Floyd Collins. His family owned the smaller Crystal Cave in Kentucky. In 1925, Floyd began exploring Mammoth Cave, hoping to discover a new entrance that might be closer to Crystal Cave. While crawling through the narrow tunnels of the nearby Sand Cave, a large rock fell on Collins's ankle, trapping him. For 17 days, rescuers attempted to save him. Miners dug a shaft through the ground. But they did not reach Collins in time, and he died in the darkness.

Floyd Collins (1887-1925) (above) peering from a cave a few days before his accident.

Škocjan Caves

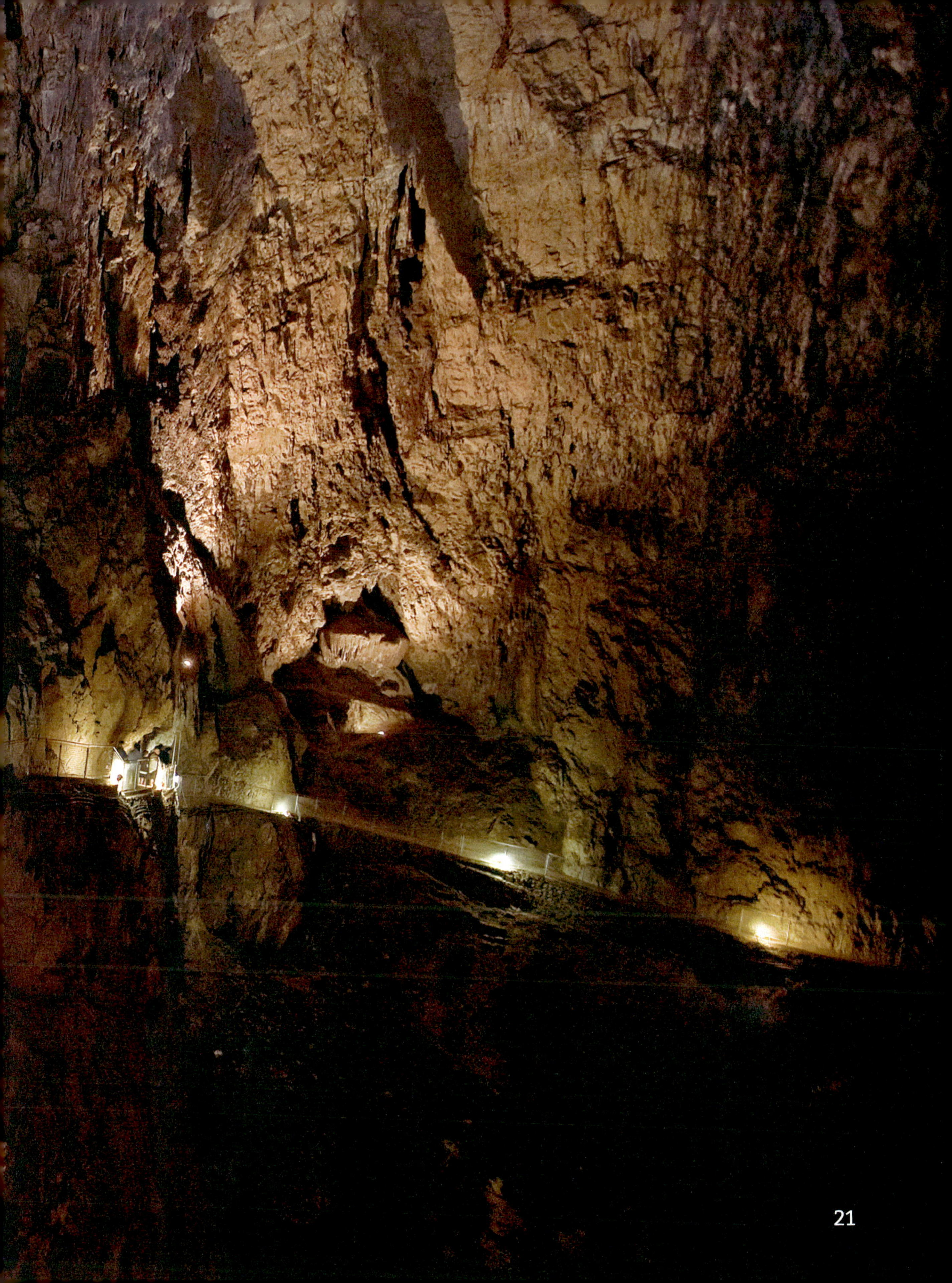

Where Are the Škocjan Caves and What's Special About Them?

Slovenia is a country next to northern Italy with a small coast on the Adriatic, an extension of the Mediterranean Sea. In the west of the country, the Reka River flows through a flat highland, or **plateau** (*pla TOH*), of **limestone** rock. Then, the river vanishes underground. Beneath the surface, the Reka has carved out a spectacular world of tunnels, halls, and cliffs: Škocjan (*shkoh TSAYHN*) Caves.

Škocjan is not nearly as big as Mammoth Cave, but some of its spaces are more dramatic. The caves are most famous for the "underground Grand Canyon," a deep *gorge* (steep valley) underneath the ground. The Reka flows at the bottom of the gorge. Visitors to the caves can cross the gorge on a bridge suspended 165 feet (50 meters) above the river.

Humans have lived around Škocjan Caves for thousands of years. The ancient Greeks and Romans knew about the caves, and so did some of the earliest mapmakers. **Geologists**—scientists who study Earth's natural features—learned much about how caves form by studying Škocjan Caves' surrounding plateau. Today, the caves are part of Škocjan Caves Park. The caves and surrounding area are valued for their rich natural and cultural heritage. The community living around the caves has long helped to maintain and protect it from damage.

A map of the Škocjan Cave system in Slovenia.

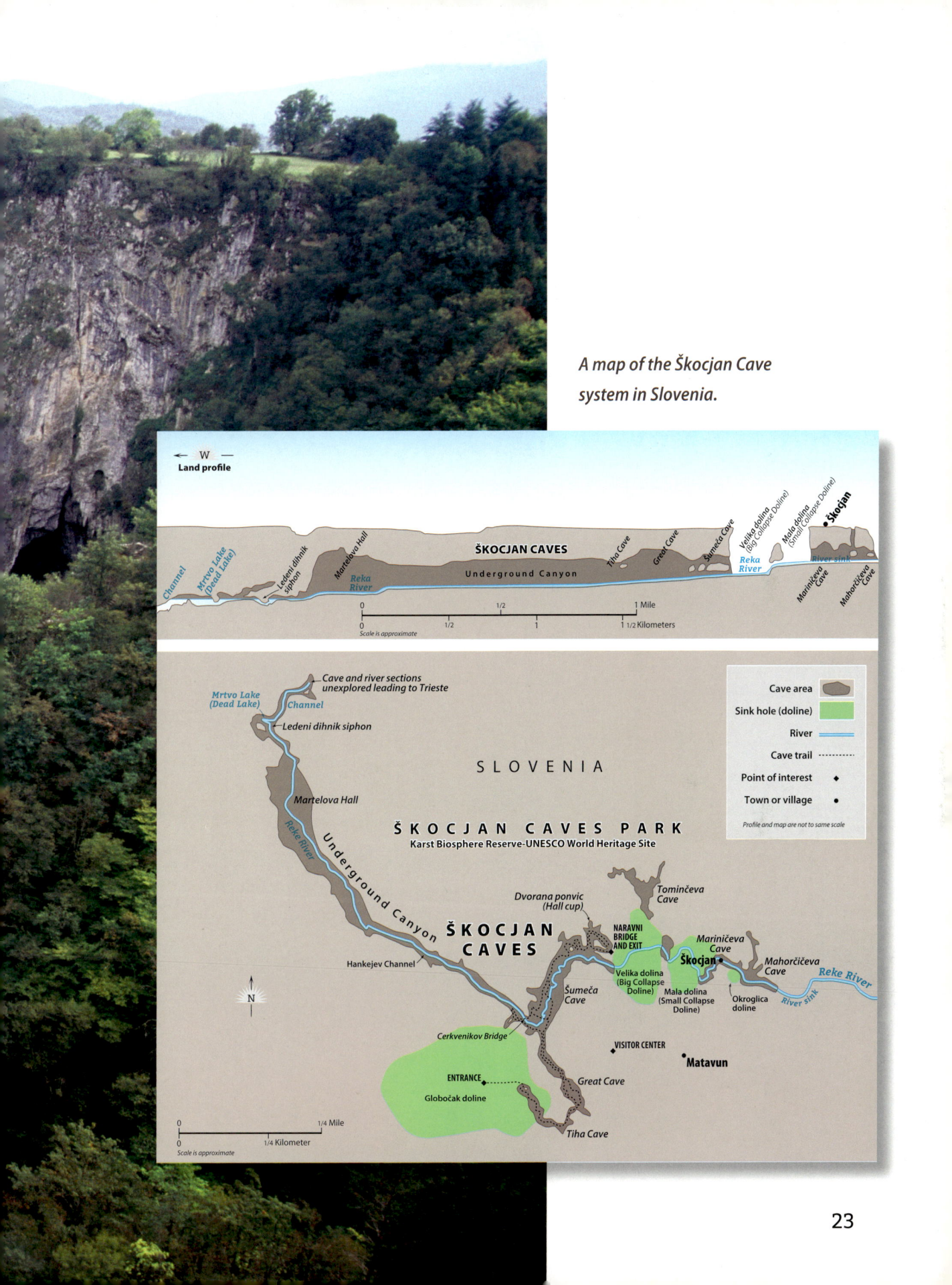

A Real-Life River Styx

Ancient Greek **myths** told of an underworld realm called **Hades** (*HAY deez*), a gloomy place where souls went after death. Much like real underground caves, the Greeks associated Hades with water. The dead supposedly traveled to Hades by way of the River Styx (*stihks*). A boatman named Charon (*KAIR uhn*) took dead souls across the river in his ferry. The Greeks buried their dead with a coin placed in the mouth to make sure the departed had money to pay Charon for the journey.

There is no real cave that leads to the mythical Hades—although Mammoth Cave does have a river named Styx. Škocjan is not Hades, either, but it is at least possible it served as an inspiration for the stories told of the land of the dead.

Archaeologists (scientists who study the remains of past human cultures) have found metal objects and evidence of *funeral rituals* (burial ceremonies) at Škocjan that date from between 1200 and 800 B.C. It is possible that people who left behind this evidence had contacts with the ancient Greeks, who did not live far away. Perhaps the Škocjan Caves inspired the ancient Greeks' descriptions of Hades.

The Reka River on its path to the underworld of Škocjan Caves.

UNDERWORLDS OF MYTH

The Greeks were not the only ancient culture to believe in a cavelike realm of the dead. The idea was common in many ancient societies around the Mediterranean Sea. The ancient Egyptians believed the dead traveled to the underworld, which was ruled by the god Osiris (oh SY rihs). The ancient Canaanites (KAY nuh nytz), who lived in what is now Israel and Lebanon, believed that the *"shades"* (spirits) of the dead went on to a gloomy underground realm. Scholars of religion and myth call such places **chthonic** (THON ihk) realms, from the Greek word *chthonios,* meaning *underground.*

The French illustrator Gustave Doré drew Charon in the image above oaring across a rough River Styx.

25

Škocjan and Geology

The Škocjan Caves have long been known to historians and mapmakers. The Greek *philosopher* (scholar interested in knowledge) and historian Posidonius (*poh sih DOHN yus*) first wrote about the caves more than 2,000 years ago.

The Škocjan Caves also played an important role in the development of modern **geology.** During the 1700's and 1800's, scientists began looking closely at the nature of the landscape surrounding Škocjan Caves. The scientists saw that much of the area consists of a kind of rock called **limestone.** Over time, water dissolved some of the rock in certain areas, forming pits, pockets, and—of course—caves.

Geologists called this special type of landscape **karst.** The word comes from Slovenia's Karst **Plateau,** where the Škocjan Caves lie. Not all karst landscapes contain caves, but many caves are found in karst areas.

Another geological term, **doline,** comes from studies of the Škocjan region. A doline is a sinkhole or bowl-shaped pit in a karst landscape. Dolines form as water wears away limestone beneath the surface. If a big enough hollow forms below, the surface rock will not have enough support. It will collapse, forming a doline. The Reka River falls into two dolines, where it then flows underground into the Škocjan Caves.

CAVE WORDS

Other caving terms—in addition to *karst* and *doline*—have a historical connection to the region near the Škocjan Caves. *Spelunker* is the word for a cave explorer, and the act of exploring a cave is *spelunking*. All words that begin with "spel" are taken from the Latin word for cave: *spelunca*. The Romans, who spoke Latin, borrowed this word from the Greeks, whose word for cave is *spelaion*.

In the Škocjan Caves (left), autumn foliage seen from a doline, a round pit into the cave. A hiker (above) stops by the Rak, a stream which disappears into the karst landscape of the Škocjan Caves.

Life in the Škocjan Caves

Ancient travelers to the Škocjan Caves must have wondered if it really was a path to the world of the dead. At the entrance, ivy and ferns cling to the rock. Further into the cave, the light dims, and there are few plants. Bats and mice occasionally make their way into the darkness. But the darkest depths of the caves must have seemed as lifeless as **Hades.**

Even in the darkest places, however, life finds a way. Škocjan Caves is home to a few kinds of **troglobites.** The most famous is the olm, pictured at right, which is also called the blind cave salamander. The olm is an amphibian, related to frogs and toads. Amphibians, including the olm, hatch from eggs laid in water.

Like many troglobites, the olm is pale. Skin grows over its eyes, though it can still sense some light—much as you can sense the sun or a bright light with your eyelids closed. The olm also has something in common with Peter Pan: it never grows up! Most amphibians change form when they become adults—for example, water-dwelling tadpoles turn into land-dwelling frogs. But the olm spends its whole life in its young, water-dwelling form. This form is well **adapted** to its dark, watery environment.

The olm was one of the first troglobites ever studied by scientists. The pale little salamander is particularly famous in Slovenia, its home country. The government has even put an image of the olm on one of the nation's coins!

Many of the bats in the Škocjan Caves are common bent-wing bats (shown above).

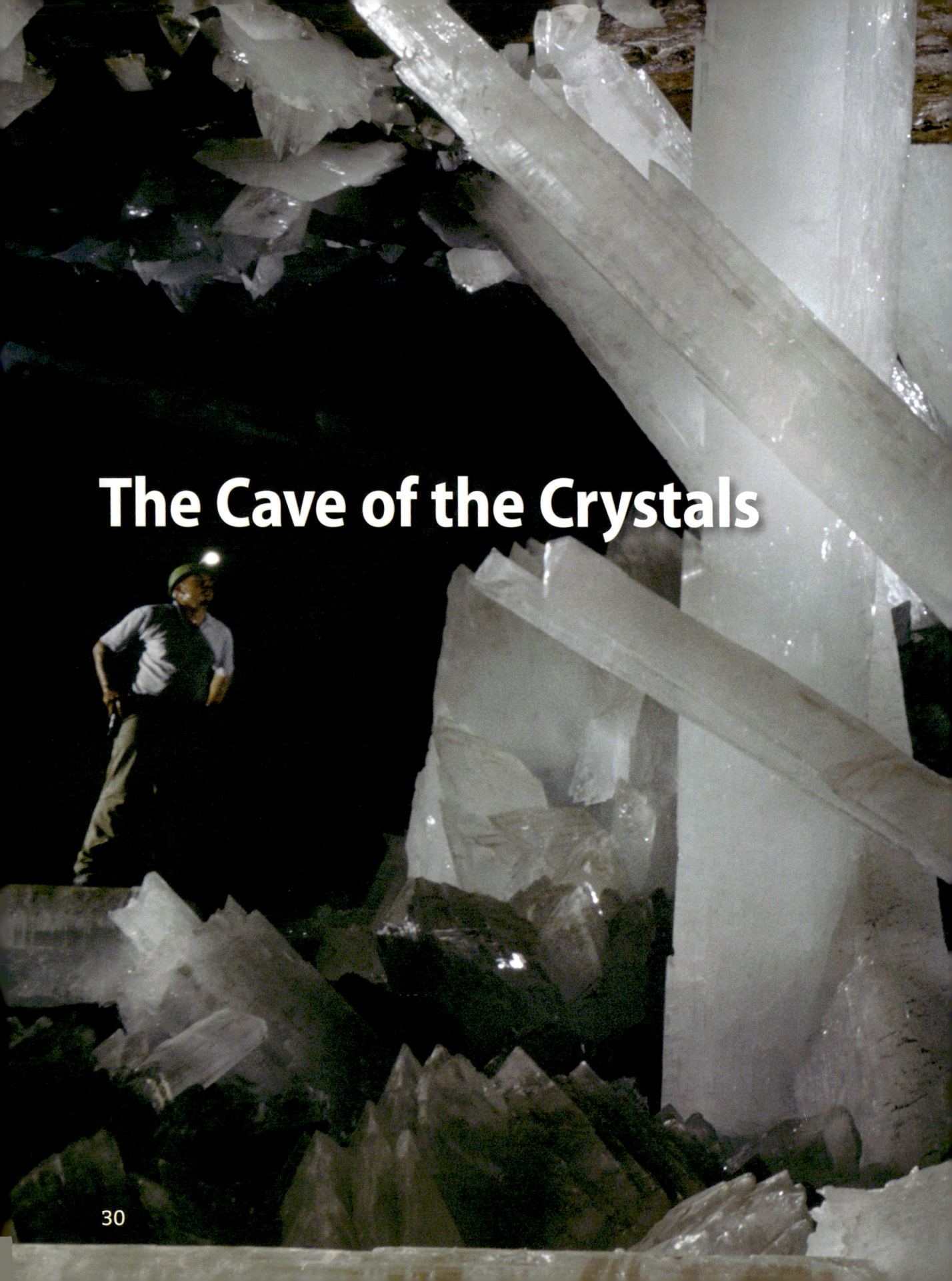

The Cave of the Crystals

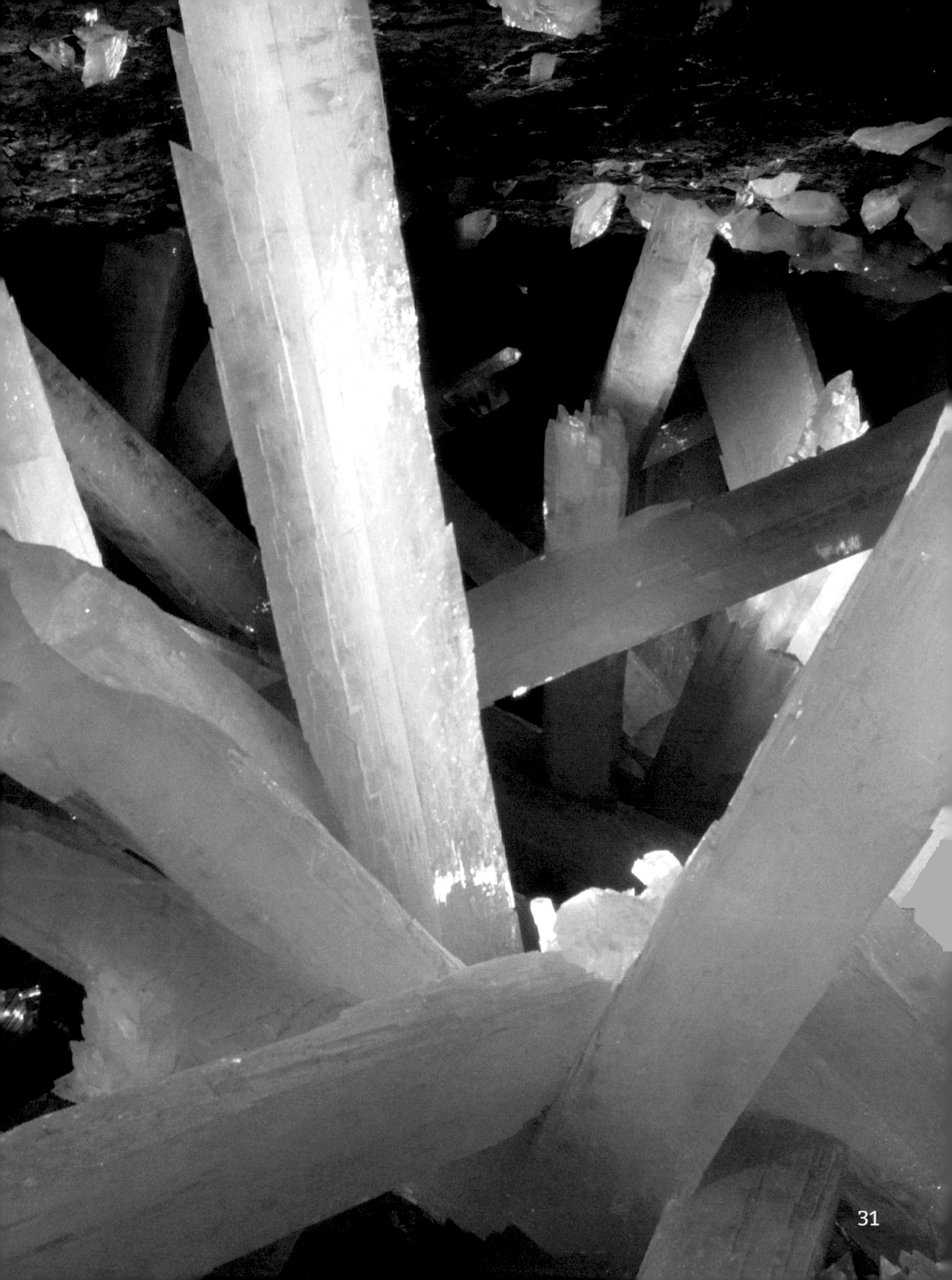

Where Is the Cave of the Crystals and What's Special About It?

The Cave of the **Crystals** lies near the town of Naica, in Chihuahua, a northern state of Mexico. Miners discovered the cave in 2000, almost 1,000 feet (300 meters) below the surface. The miners at Naica were digging for silver, zinc, and lead. Instead of these valuable minerals, the miners found something stranger—and more beautiful.

While Mammoth and Škocjan caves resemble the underworld of **myths** and legend, the Cave of the Crystals looks more like something from another planet entirely. Huge crystals jut out of the floor, ceiling, and walls, like beams from a toppled alien structure—or the teeth of a giant alien beast. The largest crystal pillar is 36 feet (11 meters) long and weighs up to 55 tons (50 metric tons).

The crystals look like ice pillars. But any actual ice would melt almost instantly in the cave's blasting heat. The temperature in the cave is a constant 136 °F (58 °C). The air inside is as humid as that of the wettest rain forest.

Cave explorers must wear protective clothing to shield them from heat as they climb over giant pillars in Mexico's Cave of the Crystals.

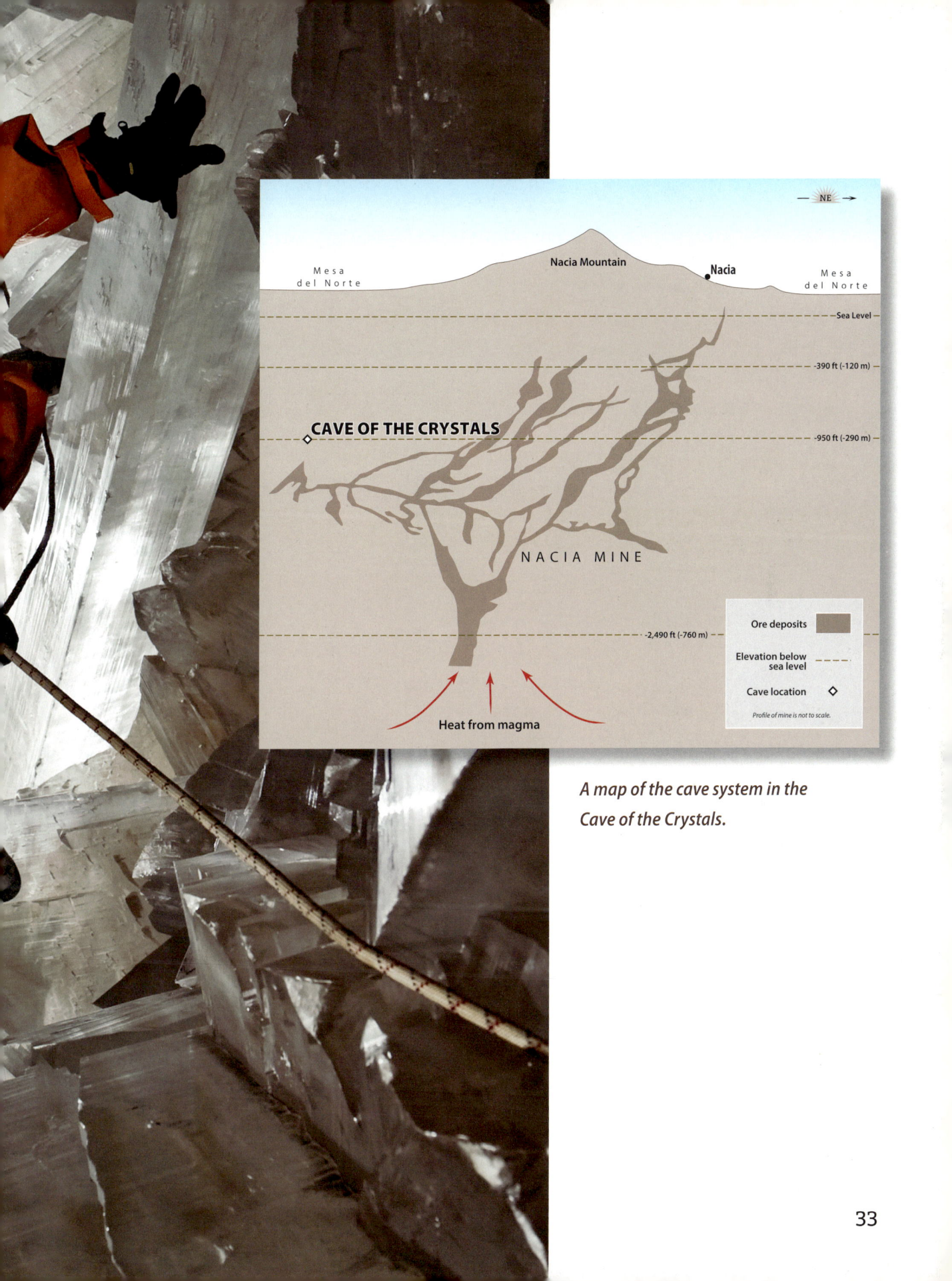

Mesa del Norte	Nacia Mountain • Nacia	Mesa del Norte

- Sea Level
- -390 ft (-120 m)

◇ **CAVE OF THE CRYSTALS** — -950 ft (-290 m)

NACIA MINE

-2,490 ft (-760 m)

↑↑↑ Heat from magma

Legend:
- Ore deposits
- Elevation below sea level
- Cave location ◇

Profile of mine is not to scale.

A map of the cave system in the Cave of the Crystals.

33

How Did Those Crystals Get So BIG?

A **crystal** is a solid substance made up of tiny bits of matter organized in a repeating pattern. Many solid substances take the form of crystals. Salt, sugar, ice, metal, and minerals found in rock—all of these things are crystals. What makes the crystals of Naica so remarkable is their enormous size.

The Naica crystals are made of a mineral called **gypsum.** Its clear crystal form is called **selenite.** Softer than a fingernail, gypsum dissolves easily in water. It is commonly found in the so-called "hard water" from many wells and springs.

How did such a common, soft mineral form towering crystals? All crystals form best in certain temperatures and other conditions. The Naica cave was once filled entirely with water. Heat from **magma**—molten rock deep beneath Earth's surface—held the water at a steady, hot temperature for many thousands of years. The water and steady hot temperature proved ideal for gypsum to form giant selenite crystals.

As part of the Naica lead and silver mining operation, miners pumped the water from the cave. The huge crystals were left behind. Eventually, the miners will allow the cave to flood again, which will help preserve the crystals.

An explorer stands among huge beams of selenite in the Cave of the Crystals.

A GIANT GEODE?

A **geode** is a hollow rock with crystals lining its inside surface. Most geodes are no bigger than a few inches or centimeters around. The crystals inside a geode form from minerals dissolved in water. Over time, the water in a geode's hollow center drains away or *evaporates* (turns from liquid to vapor) and is lost, leaving a space filled with glittering crystals. Sound familiar? Scientists think the Cave of the Crystals formed in much the same way that geodes form—only much larger!

Otherworldly Life

Compared to Mammoth or Škocjan caves, the Cave of the Crystals is much less friendly to living things. No plants or animals can survive inside, not even **troglobites.** Even with special cooling equipment, humans can only survive inside the cave for about an hour. Plus, without the mine's pumping equipment, anything living in the cave would have no air to breathe. In its natural state, the cave is flooded with hot water.

Even under these conditions, however, scientists have found traces of life: bacteria. Bacteria are *microbes* (living things too small to see without a microscope). Scientists found bacteria living in tiny air pockets inside the crystals.

Scientists call such living things **extremophiles**—meaning "lover of extremes." Extremophiles are **adapted** to live in surroundings that would instantly kill most other life. Most bacteria could never survive in the cave's harsh conditions.

The Cave of the Crystals doesn't just look like something from another world—it may hold clues about life on other worlds. Some of the conditions in the Cave of the Crystals may be similar to those found on other planets and moons. Scientists have studied the cave's extremophiles. They hope to use them to help understand how similar life forms might survive in harsh conditions on other planets.

A scientist collects gypsum crystals to test them for for bacteria inside. By studying life forms in the Cave of the Crystals, scientists hope to understand what types of things could possibly live on other planets.

37

Index

A
adaptation, 16, 17, 28, 36
amphibians, 28-29
animals, 4; Mammoth Cave, 14-17; Škocjan Cave, 28-29

B
bacteria, 36-37
bats, 14, 28-29; bent-wing, 29; Indiana, 14
beetles, cave, 16
Bishop, Stephen, 18

C
Canaanites, 25
Cave of the Crystals, 4, 30-37; crystal formation in, 32-33; features of, 32-33; life in, 36-37; maps, 5, 33
cavefish, 16-18
caves, 4-5
Charon, 24-25
chthonic realms, 25
Collins, Floyd, 19
crayfish, cave, 16
crickets, cave, 15
Crystal Cave, 19
crystals, giant, 4, 32-33, 37; origin of, 34-35

D
death, 24-25
dolines, 26-27
Doré, Gustave, 25
drapery (rocks), 11-13

E
Echo River, 8, 16, 18
Egyptians, ancient, 25
extremophiles, 36-37

F
fish, 16-18
funeral rituals, 24

G
geodes, 35
geologists, 22, 26-27
Greeks, ancient, 24-27
guano, 14
gypsum, 34, 37; flowers, 13

H
Hades, 24, 28
harvestmen, 14
helictites, 13

K
karst, 10, 26, 27
Kentucky, 4, 8

L
landforms, 5
life: Cave of the Crystals, 36-37; extraterrestrial, 36-37; Mammoth Cave, 14-17; Škocjan Cave, 28-29
limestone, 10, 22, 26

M
magma, 34
Mammoth Cave, 4, 6-19, 24, 32, 36; animals of, 14-17; exploring, 18-19; features of, 8-9; formation of, 10-13; maps, 5, 9
Mammoth Cave National Park, 8, 9
Mexico, 4, 32
microbes, 36-37
millipedes, cave, 17
myths, 4, 24-25, 32

N
Naica, Mexico, 32, 34
Native Americans, 18

O
olms, 28-29
Osiris, 25

P
plants, 28
Posidonius, 26

R
Rak (stream), 27
Reka River, 22-26
rock formations. *See* speleothems
Romans, ancient, 27

S
salamanders, blind cave, 28-29
saltpeter, 18
selenite, 34
shrimp, cave, 16, 17
Škocjan Cave, 4, 20-29, 32, 36; features of, 22-23; geology and, 26-27; life in, 28-29; maps, 5, 23; myth and, 24-25
Škocjan Caves Park, 22, 23
Slovenia, 4, 22, 26, 28
speleologists, 9
speleothems, 8, 10-13
spelunkers, 8, 12, 18-19, 27; dangers for, 19
stalactites, 12
stalagmites, 12
Styx, River, 24-25

T
troglobites, 4, 36; Mammoth Cave, 8, 15-17; Škocjan Cave, 28-29

U
underworld, 24-25, 32

W
War of 1812, 18
water tables, 10, 13

+
551.447 K

Kenis, Daniel.
Worlds beneath our feet /
Freed-Montrose NONFICTION
05/17